STORIES OF THE
Great Composers

Short Sessions on the Lives and Music of the
Great Composers with Imaginary Stories Based on Fact
FOR ELEMENTARY STUDENTS

It is important that young students learn about the lives of the great composers who have enriched our lives with beautiful music.

STORIES OF THE GREAT COMPOSERS is designed to give elementary students a glimpse into the composer's life, character and music.

There are 12 composer units in this book. Each unit contains:

* a picture of the composer with a short biography

* an imaginary story based on fact about an event in the composer's life, family or music

* a list of three important compositions by the composer, as well as a short description of the composition found on the optional accompanying compact disc

* a question and answer page for review in the form of a puzzle or matching game.

In the back of the book there is a composer game in which clues are given to identify each composer.

Each unit is designed to be completed in a 15–20 minute session. The session may be extended with the addition of listening and other activities.

A CD recording of the suggested listening is included. The recording contains one composition by each composer, for a variety of mediums, including piano, orchestra and band.

JUNE MONTGOMERY AND MAURICE HINSON

Alfred

Photos: Archiv für Kunst und Geschichte, London

Opera Singer Photo: © Corbis Corp.

Contents

Johann Sebastian Bach ...a composer from GERMANY who lived during the BAROQUE period of music...

Johann Sebastian Bach was born in Germany in 1685.

Going back many generations, the Bach family was known to be very musical—some played violin, some oboe, some organ and harpsichord. Others were music copyists. Though music was important to the Bach family, many of them worked as bakers, cobblers, weavers or hat makers to help support their families.

Bach's father, Johann Ambrosius, taught Bach to play the violin. His older brother, Johann Christoph, taught him organ, harpsichord and clavichord.

When Bach was nearly 10 years old, his parents died. He and his 13-year-old brother, Josef, went to live with Christoph and his wife. For the next five years, Bach lived with his brother, attended school and became an outstanding student. When he was 15, he left Johann Christoph's home and went to Lüneberg to become a choirboy at St. Michael's Church.

In his lifetime Bach was known more for his excellent organ playing than for composing. Many years after he died, Felix Mendelssohn discovered Bach's compositions. He arranged for Bach's music to be played, because he wanted others to hear Bach's truly great music. He organized the compositions into 60 volumes of music.

Bach died in 1750 at the age of 65.

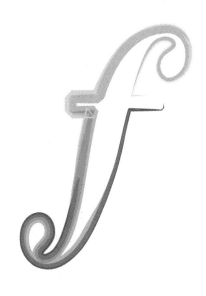

The Bach Family of Musicians

Johann Sebastian Bach, the great musician, sat at his harpsichord working very hard on a composition.

He was the organist and choir director for his church and he was writing an anthem called *Jesu, Joy of Man's Desiring*. This piece was to be a part of a cantata for a special service.

He was concentrating so hard that he didn't notice the gentle tugging on his sleeve, until it became more insistent.

He heard three small voices saying, "Papa, we are hungry! May we have a snack?"

Pretending to be angry, Bach turned to face them and said with a deep voice and frown, "What? You are interrupting your papa's composing for a mere 'something to eat'?"

Then with a laugh he said, "Go ahead to the kitchen, I'll be right there!"

The children laughed as they hurried to sit at the long kitchen table. Soon their papa came and sliced a loaf of bread, buttered it and spread each piece with honey.

As the children were eating their snack, Johann Christian said, "Papa, please tell us about the time you walked so far to hear the great organist play."

"Once when I was in school," Bach began, "I heard about a wonderful organist and composer named Johann Adam

Bach and his wife, Maria Barbara, had seven children. With his second wife, Anna Magdalena, he had thirteen children—TWENTY children in all! Sadly, only nine of them lived to be adults.

Reinken. I wanted so badly to hear him play. When I heard that he was playing a concert at a church in Hamburg, I decided that I would get there no matter what! I had no money to pay for a ride, so I packed a lunch and started walking. When I arrived in Hamburg, four days later, I was exhausted. However, that did not prevent me from going straight to the church to listen to Mr. Reinken practice. Oh! What beautiful music I heard! It filled my heart and soul. I wanted to play like that!"

"But papa," said little Johanna Carolina, "everyone says that you are the very best organist they have ever heard! Maybe someone will walk a very long way to hear you play!"

"Well," said Bach, "I have practiced a lot of hours since those days."

"When will our next Bach family day be, papa?" asked Johann Christoph Frederick.

Bach smiled and said, "It will be next month. You will all be old enough to play

Bach's wife and older children helped him copy music for different instruments and for his students.

your instruments with us, except you, little Johanna. If you keep practicing, you may be able to play next year.

"Your uncles, older brothers and cousins will be here," he continued. "They will bring their different instruments. We will have such a good time playing old and new pieces. We'll have a wonderful meal and no one will want to go home! I can't wait, can you?"

"Will it be like our family gathering each night at evening prayers, papa?"

"Yes," said Bach as he gave each child a hug, "that reminds me, aren't you supposed to play your violins tonight? Come, all of you, let's go practice. You too, Johanna!"

Soon happy voices and beautiful music filled the room.

For his oldest son, Wilhelm Friedemann, Bach composed a book called **Little Book for the Keyboard.** He used this book to teach his students and his own children to play the harpsichord.

Important Compositions

Toccata and Fugue in D Minor, BWV 565

St. Matthew Passion, BWV 244

Brandenburg Concertos

1 Jesu, Joy of Man's Desiring

Jesu, Joy of Man's Desiring is one of Bach's best known pieces. It has a lovely melody and a flowing accompaniment. This piece, originally written for chorus and orchestra, is from Bach's Cantata No. 147. A popular piece called Joy uses this melody and accompaniment. The example you will hear is played on an organ.

Bach Match

Draw a line to connect the circle with the square that matches.

The country where Bach was born

Baroque

Germany

The instrment Bach's father taught him to play

Violin

Twenty

The number of children Bach had

The musical period in which Bach lived

Johann Sebastian Bach (at the keyboard) and his family

Franz Joseph Haydn

... a composer from AUSTRIA who lived during the CLASSICAL period of music ...

Franz Joseph Haydn was born in Austria in 1732.

His parents were poor. His father fixed wheels on carriages, and his mother was a cook. They were a musical family. His father sang and played the harp.

It was said that when Joseph was just a small boy, he picked up two sticks and pretended to play the fiddle.

His parents knew that Joseph had an unusual talent in music, but they did not have the money to train him properly. Fortunately, a cousin solved the problem by taking the six-year-old Joseph to live with him and giving him the music training that he needed.

Two years later, because of his beautiful voice, he was invited to join the famous boys choir at the St. Stephen Cathedral in Vienna. Here he received the best possible education at no expense to his parents.

Haydn shared a long friendship with Mozart, whom he greatly admired.

Haydn was religious. At the beginning of many of his compositions he wrote the words, "In the Name of the Lord."

He died in 1809 at the age of 77.

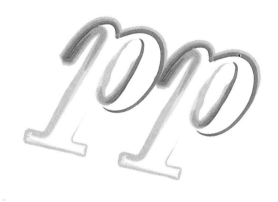

A Farewell Surprise

The orchestra rehearsal was not going well. After a poor performance of several pieces, Haydn closed his music and asked, "What is wrong? Your playing is flat and dull. We need to have more life and energy in our performance and you are not even paying attention to the music!"

The orchestra members looked uneasily at each other. Finally, Anton, the cellist, spoke. "We are so tired," he said. "We were supposed to go home two months ago, and Prince Esterházy has kept us here too long."

"We miss our families. We want to see our wives and children," added Karl, the horn player.

"You are right," said Maestro Haydn. "We all need a vacation. Rehearsal is dismissed. I will let the Prince know that we need to go home."

The orchestra, under Haydn's direction, had become one of the finest orchestras in Europe. When Prince Esterházy went to his summer home, he insisted that the orchestra come also. He wanted them to provide entertainment for his family and guests by giving concerts and playing for dances.

Haydn thought about all of these things as he walked slowly back to his room. Suddenly, he stopped! He had an idea. He began to walk quickly with a broad smile on his face.

He hurried to his room, and with manuscript paper and pen, he began composing. He worked many hours. Finally, he put down his pen and with a twinkle in his eye and a hearty laugh, he said, "I hope this works!"

Haydn was so excited he could hardly wait until the next rehearsal. When the orchestra had gathered to practice, he leaned over the music stand and quietly told the orchestra his plan. The orchestra members looked a little puzzled as Haydn gave them copies of his new symphony. Soon everyone was happy and ready to practice with spirit and attention.

On the night of the concert, the audience was quiet as the orchestra began to play. The audience listened intently as the orchestra played with life and beauty.

> Young Joseph loved pranks and jokes. He showed his good sense of humor in many of his compositions.

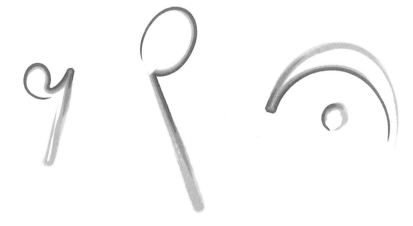

The time had finally come for the last piece on the program. With a wink and a smile, Haydn raised his hands and the orchestra began to play. At first, all of the orchestra played together, and then one by one members took their instruments, picked up the candles on the music stands and left the stage. By the end of the symphony only Haydn himself and two violinists remained. The audience didn't know what to think! Then the Prince realized what the performance of *The Farewell Symphony* was trying to tell him.

With his keen sense of humor, and his great talent as a composer, Haydn was able to convince the Prince that it was time to let his orchestra go home to be with their families. The very next day the happy orchestra members left the palace to go home to Vienna.

Haydn is considered the father of the symphony and the string quartet.

He was so well liked that Mozart and others among his many friends affectionately called him "Papa Haydn."

Important Compositions

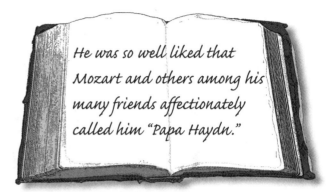

Piano Sonata in D Major, Hob. XVI:37

The Creation (Oratorio), Hob. XXI:2

The Emperor's Hymn
(Austrian National Anthem)

2

Symphony No. 94 in G Major, **Hob. I:94 ("The Surprise"), Second Movement**
Haydn had noticed that the London audiences "slept peacefully during the slow movements" of his symphonies. To correct this situation Haydn wrote this symphony, which became very popular. There is a quiet section of the slow movement, and then, suddenly, the full orchestra with all the big drums plays a very loud chord. All those who were sleeping awakened with a jerk! Surprise!

Haydn Word Search

Look down or across to find words that will complete the sentences below. Circle the words.

```
B  S  E  H  M  O  Z  A  R  T
J  U  X  K  S  N  T  G  S  H
A  R  D  P  Q  F  B  O  M  D
F  P  M  W  A  V  Y  C  Q  P
P  R  G  E  U  Y  L  T  J  A
H  I  B  S  D  M  Z  C  U  P
C  S  T  I  X  A  R  F  W  A
L  E  K  N  Z  E  S  I  N  J
D  R  Q  C  H  V  B  K  F  L
E  O  G  A  U  S  T  R  I  A
```

Franz Joseph Haydn was born in the country of _____.

Haydn had a long friendship with _____,
    whose music he greatly admired.

Haydn wrote a symphony with a very loud chord in it to wake everyone who might
    be sleeping. It is called the _____ symphony.

Haydn was affectionately called "_____ Haydn"
    by many of his friends.

Ludwig van Beethoven

... a composer from GERMANY who lived during the LATE CLASSICAL–EARLY ROMANTIC period of music ...

Ludwig van Beethoven was born in Germany in 1770.

He came from a long line of musicians that extended back to his great-grandfather.

Ludwig's father began teaching him piano and violin when he was four years old. He already showed promise of musical talent, and his father wanted him to be a successful child prodigy like Mozart. At about the age of ten, Beethoven began piano lessons with Christian Gottlob Neefe, his first important piano teacher.

Beethoven became known as one of the greatest pianists of his day. He played an important role in the development of piano music.

Beethoven began losing his hearing when he was 30 years old and was completely deaf by the time he was 50. However, he continued to write down the music he heard in his head.

Beethoven died in 1827 at the age of 56.

Beethoven in the woods

A Walk in the Woods

"Quickly, Karl," Nicholas called as he ran toward the woods. "If we hurry, we can get to our hideout before mother sees us and wants us to do more chores."

"Coming!" said Karl as he followed close behind.

Soon they came to their favorite tree and climbed up to their look out. They often pretended to be pirates or scouts looking for the enemy.

"Sh…sh…sh…," whispered Karl, "I hear someone coming." Both boys looked through the leaves of the tree to see who was coming down the path into the woods.

"Oh, it's Herr Beethoven," said Nick. "See, he has his notebook with him as he always does."

Beethoven was walking slowly through the woods. He was beginning to lose his hearing and he seemed to listen very carefully to the birds calling and the brook babbling as it flowed by. It was as if he were storing up all the lovely sounds of nature so that he could hear them in his mind when he could no longer hear them with his ears.

The movement of the leaves caught Beethoven's eye. He looked up and called, "Hello there, young fellows! How is the scouting today?"

The boys laughed and hurried down from the tree. "We don't see much today, Herr Beethoven. There are just some sheep in the pasture and some dogs barking."

"Well then, good day to you! Keep up the good watch!" said Beethoven as he continued on his way. The boys watched as he walked by the brook, through the woods and into the village square where the band was practicing and some villagers were dancing in the street. Often he would stop, take out his notebook and write notes and melodies on the page.

The sound of thunder began to rumble in the distance. It was getting late, so the brothers returned home.

A little over a year later as their mother was putting Karl and Nicholas to bed, she said, "Boys, you are 10 and 12 years old now. Would you like to attend a concert? Herr Beethoven's new symphony will be performed tomorrow night, along with some of his other compositions!"

"Oh! Yes, we would really like that!" said the excited boys.

The next night at the concert as the beautiful sounds of Symphony No. 6 (The Pastoral) filled the auditorium, Karl and Nicholas looked at each other. Much to their surprise and delight they heard sounds like birds calling, the babbling of a brook, a fierce thunderstorm and a village dance.

Beethoven studied music for a while with Franz Joseph Haydn.

They smiled a secret smile at each other. They knew that they had been present when the great composer, Herr Beethoven, had written ideas in his notebook for this beautiful symphony.

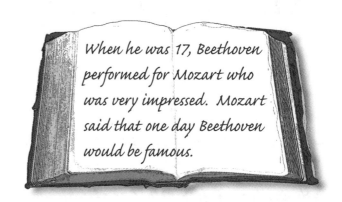

When he was 17, Beethoven performed for Mozart who was very impressed. Mozart said that one day Beethoven would be famous.

Important Compositions

Symphony No. 1 in C Major, Op. 21

Symphony No. 2 in D Major, Op. 36

Symphony No. 3 in E-flat Major, Op. 55 ("Eroica")

Symphony No. 4 in B-flat Major, Op. 60

Symphony No. 5 in C minor, Op. 67

Symphony No. 6 in F Major, Op. 68 ("Pastoral")

Symphony No. 7 in A Major, Op. 92

Symphony No. 8 in F Major, Op. 93

Symphony No. 9 in D Minor, Op. 125 ("Choral")

Piano Sonata in C-sharp Minor, Op. 27, No. 2 ("Moonlight")

Für Elise, WoO 59

Piano Concerto No. 5 in E-flat Major, Op. 73 ("Emperor")

 3

***Symphony No. 6 in F Major*, Op. 68 ("Pastoral"), Second Movement**

The *Pastoral Symphony* was completed in the summer of 1808. It was first performed the following December. The movements are described as follows:

Movement 1: Waking of cheerful feelings on arrival in the country
Movement 2: Scene by a brook
Movement 3: Merry making of country folk
Movement 4: A storm
Movement 5: Song of shepherds with joy and gratitude after the storm

BEETHOVEN PUZZLE

Draw a line through the incorrect answer.

Ludwig van Beethoven was born in (France, Germany).

Beethoven's Symphony No. 6 is also known as the (Pastoral, Farewell).

In later life, Beethoven was completely (blind, deaf).

Beethoven wrote (nine, thirteen) symphonies.

Beethoven was admired for his talent playing the (trumpet, piano).

Color Beethoven.

Franz Schubert

...a composer from AUSTRIA who lived during the LATE CLASSICAL–EARLY ROMANTIC period of music...

Franz Schubert was born in Austria in 1797.

His father was a schoolmaster and played the violin and cello.

Franz's father taught him to play the violin. His older brother, Ignaz taught him piano. Franz was such an eager student that his teachers had trouble keeping ahead of him. He seemed to already know what they were going to say.

Schubert was a very friendly, happy and likable person. He had many friends. They gathered in the evenings to hear Schubert play his music and to enjoy hearing some of the best singers perform his songs. These evening parties were known as "Schubertiades." Everyone had a good time listening, laughing, playing games and dancing.

Schubert wrote 8 symphonies, the best known being *Symphony No. 8*, which is also known as the *Unfinished Symphony*.

Schubert is best remembered for his beautiful songs. He is sometimes called the "Master of the German Song."

Schubert died in 1828 at the age of 31.

An Evening with Schubert

The furniture was pulled back to the walls and the room was filled with young couples. Some were dancing, some were playing cards in the corner and others were watching from their chairs against the walls.

"Tubby, more music! More music!" the dancers called as the piece ended.

Franz Peter Schubert, fondly called "Tubby" or "Franzl" by his friends, sat at the piano, playing his compositions for those who were dancing. Franz really liked these evening parties. His friends called the gatherings "Schubertiades," because Schubert's music was the center of the activities. He composed for them to dance, to sing and to perform.

"Let's listen for a while," said one of the ladies, as she tried to catch her breath. "That last dance was very fast."

"A very good idea!" agreed the other dancers. "Let's have a song! Vogl, sing for us," said Franz from the piano. "Vogl, Vogl! Sing for us!" the others joined in.

Johann Michael Vogl, a wealthy, dignified man was a good friend of Franz's. He had a wonderful baritone voice and was a popular singer in the theater. He enjoyed singing the songs composed by his friend. He especially enjoyed singing at the Schubertiades. It didn't take much to persuade him to come to the piano.

The dancers and card players moved to sit in the chairs. Vogl began to sing. He had selected *Ave Maria* by Schubert to sing. There was not another sound in the room as he sang. The audience was spellbound.

When he finished, they shouted, "More, More!"

"Any requests?" asked Vogl.

> When he was a boy, Schubert sang in the Imperial Choir. When his voice changed, he wrote in his choir book that Franz had "crowed" for the last time.

"Please sing *Serenade* by Franz," one of the ladies said. "Oh, yes! That's my favorite too," said another.

A Schubertiad, with Franz Schubert seated at the piano

When he finished, there was even more applause.

"Now something different," said Franz. "I have written a duet for piano. Who will come and play with me?"

Several friends volunteered and Franz picked one. The composition was called *March Militaire*. It was a lively and rhythmic march. Everyone loved it!

"It's your best piece yet," said Josef, one of Schubert's friends. "One day it will be famous!"

After more dancing and games, the friends went home, knowing that there would be many more pleasant evenings like this one.

"Johann, please stay a minute," said Franz. "I want you to take this new song home with you, look it over and tell me what you think."

Vogl took the manuscript with him. He liked it very much, but it was too low for his voice. He worked very hard and transposed the song into a key that he could sing.

Several weeks later, he took the song back to Schubert. Franz looked at it and said, "This is a really good song! Who is the composer?"

"Look at it again," said Johann with a laugh.

"Oh! It is my composition that you have transposed!" said Franz. He had forgotten his own song!

The two friends laughed as they took the composition to the piano to play and sing.

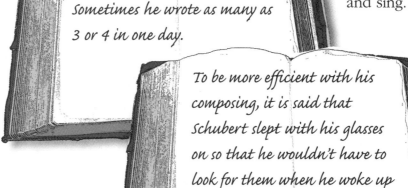

Schubert wrote over 600 songs. Sometimes he wrote as many as 3 or 4 in one day.

To be more efficient with his composing, it is said that Schubert slept with his glasses on so that he wouldn't have to look for them when he woke up in the morning.

Important Compositions

20 Piano Sonatas

600 songs, favorites include: *Serenade; Ave Maria; Hark, Hark the Lark; Who is Sylvia?*

Symphony No. 8 in B Minor, D. 759 ("Unfinished")

Valses Sentimentales, D. 779, Nos. 1, 25, 26

These waltzes are typical of the kind of dances that Schubert might have played at the Schubertiades. Their lilting rhythms makes them enjoyable pieces to hear and play, and they are certainly appropriate for accompanying a dance.

Schubert Crossword

Complete the sentences. Write the answers in the blanks of the puzzle.

1. Franz Schubert wrote over 600 ________________.

2. When he was a boy, Franz sang in the Imperial ______________.

3. Franz was popular with his friends who nicknamed him "______________."

4. Franz's ______________ attended his evening music gatherings, known as "Schubertiades."

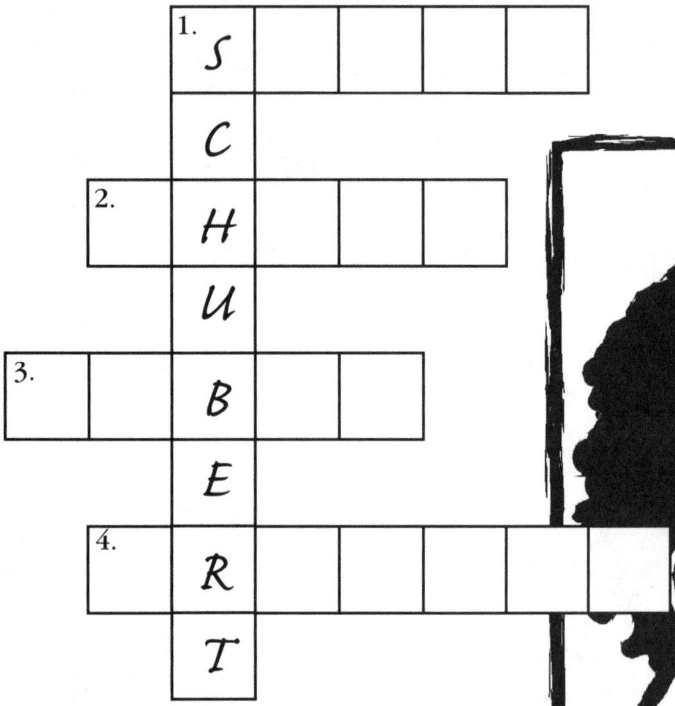

Color Schubert.

Felix Mendelssohn and Fanny Mendelssohn Hensel

. . . brother and sister composers from GERMANY who lived during the ROMANTIC period of music . . .

Fanny Mendelssohn was born in 1805 and Felix Mendelssohn was born in 1809 in Germany.

They had a wealthy, loving family with all the advantages of a very fine education. All of the children, Fanny, Felix, Rebeka and Paul, had lessons in math, art, literature and language as well as musical instruments of all types.

Their parents were the first to teach music to the children, then they hired the finest teachers available.

Both Fanny and Felix became outstanding pianists. Sometimes when people would compliment Felix on his playing, he would say, "You should hear my sister!"

On Fanny's 13th birthday, she performed from memory for her father the 24 preludes from the *Well-Tempered Clavier, Book 1* by Johann Sebastian Bach.

As adults, both Fanny and Felix were happily married and each had several children. However, they remained best friends their entire lives.

Fanny Mendelssohn died in 1847 as she was practicing one of Felix' compositions. She was 41 years old. Felix died the same year at age 38.

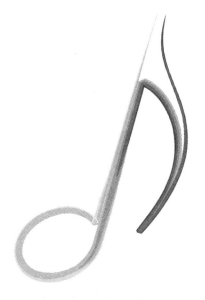

A Brother and Sister Duet

"Felix, there you are!" said his older sister, Fanny, as she came into the studio. "I've been looking all over the house for you!"

"What's up, Fanny? You sound so excited! What's going on?" asked Felix as he put down his brush and stopped work on his painting.

"I have good news, Felix! I have found a wonderful play for us to perform at our Sunday gathering.

"Good for you!" said Felix. "Let me clean my hands and we'll look at it!"

Both heads were soon bent over the play by Shakespeare, *A Midsummer Night's Dream*.

"This is wonderful!" exclaimed the excited Felix. "It's perfect! You shall be Hermia and I shall be Lysander."

"I shall not!" said Fanny. "Lysander and Hermia are in love. It would take a lot of acting to pretend to be in love with my brother!"

"Oh, but you are perfect for the part,

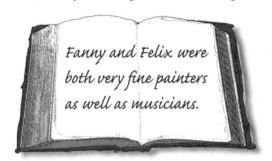

Fanny and Felix were both very fine painters as well as musicians.

and maybe Rebeka can be one of the pixies. Do you think Paul is too young to play the mischievous Puck?"

They continued planning until all was set for the first rehearsal.

The children were required to get up for their studies at five o'clock each morning. On Sundays, the Mendelssohn home was a meeting place for family, friends and guests to share music, dancing and plays. It was for one of these gatherings that Felix and Fanny were planning to perform *A Midsummer Night's Dream*.

They did perform it and it was such a success that Felix decided to write music for it. He was only 17 years old when he composed the *Overture to A Midsummer Night's Dream*. He wrote the composition for piano duet, and he and Fanny performed it at another of the Sunday gatherings.

The audience was amazed and thrilled with the composition. Word soon spread and the overture was performed often and became very popular.

Some of Fanny's compositions were published under her brother's name.

One day, many years later, Felix had a message from King Wilhelm. He sent word for Felix to come to the palace right away.

When Felix arrived at the palace, the royal court poet said, "I have just translated the Shakespeare play, *A Midsummer Night's Dream* from the English language and the king wants you to write music for the play."

Felix's thoughts went back to that happy time when he and Fanny had performed at the Sunday gathering in his parents' home. It didn't take long for him to write music to add to the overture he had written 17 years before. All the scenes of the mythical forest, the pixies, the donkey and the royal wedding were soon transformed into beautiful "story-telling" music.

The first performance of *A Midsummer Night's Dream* with Mendelssohn's music was given in the theater of the New Palace at Potsdam, just outside of Berlin.

Before he had them performed, Felix always sent his compositions to Fanny for her opinion and advice. She was especially proud of this composition, because she remembered how it all got started.

It became one of Mendelssohn's most famous compositions.

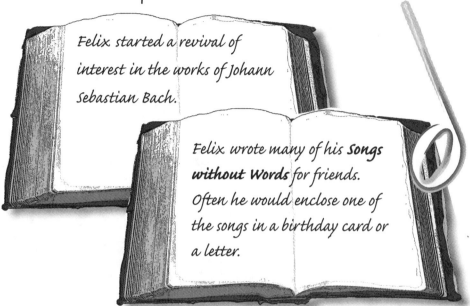

Felix started a revival of interest in the works of Johann Sebastian Bach.

*Felix wrote many of his **Songs without Words** for friends. Often he would enclose one of the songs in a birthday card or a letter.*

Important Compositions

Fanny is best known for her songs. They both wrote many *Songs without Words* for piano.

Felix wrote the oratorio *Elijah*, Op. 70.

Felix wrote the *Violin Concerto in E Minor*, Op. 64

5 *The Wedding March* from *A Midsummer Night's Dream*
by Felix Mendelssohn.
This march is one of Mendelssohn's most popular pieces. It first became popular to use in weddings in 1858, when it was performed at the wedding of an English Princess in London. Since that time, this overture has been played at weddings all over the world.

6 *Farewell to Rome*
by Fanny Mendelssohn Hensel.
This piece was probably composed in 1840, following Fanny's first visit to Italy. It is one of her *Songs without Words*.

Mendelssohn Match

Draw a line to connect the circle with the square that matches.

Fanny and her husband Wilhelm Hensel

At age 13, performed from memory the preludes from the **Well-Tempered Clavier, Book 1** by J. S. Bach

Felix Mendelssohn

Germany

The country where Fanny and Felix were born

Johann Sebastian Bach

Fanny Mendelssohn

Felix started a revival of this great composer's music

Wrote the oratorio, **Elijah**, Op. 70

Frédéric François Chopin ... a composer from POLAND who lived during the ROMANTIC period of music...

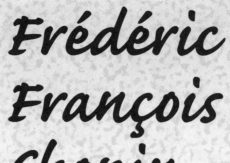

Frédéric François Chopin was born in Poland in 1810.

Frédéric's father, Nicolas, was a schoolteacher. His mother, Justyna, was the cousin of a countess. They were both musical and well educated. They were very supportive parents who gave their children a well-rounded education.

As a child prodigy, Chopin's genius was compared to that of the great Wolfgang Amadeus Mozart.

As a young boy, Frédéric often played for the Grand Duke. When he was depressed, Frédéric's music seemed to soothe the duke's nerves.

By the time Frédéric was 17, he was known as the best pianist and composer in Poland.

He loved his native country with a passion. Many of his compositions include folk tunes and songs. That is one of the reasons that the people loved his music.

In 1829, while Chopin was successfully performing concerts in Paris, the Russians invaded his home country. He remained in Paris and was never able to return to his beloved Poland.

In 1849, at the age of 39, Chopin died in Paris, France.

Color Chopin.

A Polish Genius

In the kitchen, Frédéric's parents were talking.

"But Nicolas, he is only four years old! That is too young to be taking piano lessons," said Frédéric's mother.

"You are right Justyna, but he shows such an exceptional interest in music! We must watch him carefully and be sure to get him a teacher at the right time. In the meantime, I will continue to help him a little and so can Louise."

Sounds of a Bach menuet were heard in the living room. Frédéric's seven-year-old sister, Louise, came running to the kitchen door.

"Mama and papa, come and listen to Frédéric! I played the menuet twice and now he can play it!"

The astonished parents listened as little four-year-old Frédéric played note for note the Bach menuet that Louise had played earlier.

They clapped with pleasure as Frédéric and Louise took a bow. "After all, I taught him," said Louise.

Two years passed and Frédéric's parents knew that the time had come for him to begin piano lessons.

Frédéric was drawing with his sisters, Louise, Isabella and Emily, when his father came to the door.

"Come Frédéric," said his father, "I have a surprise for you!"

Frédéric was so happy and excited to find Mr. Albert Zywny, a piano teacher, waiting for him.

As they worked together, it was obvious to Mr. Zywny that Frédéric was a genius. Not only could he play beautifully, but he began to compose his own pieces.

"Listen to my polonaise," said the seven-year-old Frédéric to his teacher as he began his lesson. Mr. Zywny thought it was a wonderful piece and as a surprise he had it published for Frédéric. It was Frédéric's first published composition, *Polonaise in G Minor.*

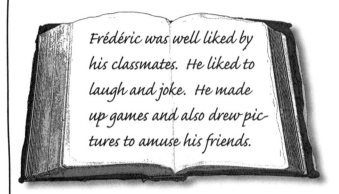

Frédéric was well liked by his classmates. He liked to laugh and joke. He made up games and also drew pictures to amuse his friends.

"Now it is time for you to give a concert," said Mr. Zywny at a lesson the next year.

The eight-year-old Frédéric, dressed in a black velvet jacket, a huge white lace collar, short pants and white stockings was taken in a carriage to Radziwill Palace.

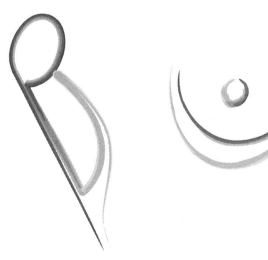

The audience was spellbound as he played a difficult concerto.

When he came home he said, "Guess what, mother? They liked the beautiful white collar you made for me!"

After the concert, coaches could often be seen coming to the door of the Chopin home to take the young Frédéric to their homes and castles to perform for these wealthy people and their friends.

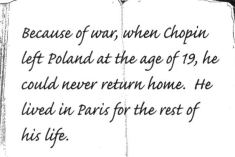

Because of war, when Chopin left Poland at the age of 19, he could never return home. He lived in Paris for the rest of his life.

When Frédéric was 19, he began a tour of several large cities in Europe. Before he left, some friends gave him a jar of Polish soil, so that he could always remember the country he loved. He treasured this gift and kept it with him always. After his death, this soil was sprinkled on his grave.

Most of Chopin's compositions were for solo piano.

Important Compositions

Polonaise Militaire, Op. 40, No. 1
Revolutionary Étude, Op. 10, No. 12
Raindrop Prélude, Op. 28, No. 15

♪7 *Polonaise in G Minor*

The polonaise was a national dance in Poland, but Chopin made the polonaise a symbol of Polish heroism. This polonaise was Chopin's first published piece, written when he was just 7 years old. It was considered by many to be a work of genius.

Chopin Word Search

Look down or across to find words that will complete the sentences below. Circle the words.

```
P  E  I  P  L  A  J  C  O  G
I  A  K  O  B  S  W  M  U  F
A  M  G  L  D  Y  F  Q  P  M
N  C  U  A  E  H  N  A  X  R
O  S  O  N  D  C  L  T  O  I
E  L  X  D  M  J  Z  E  Z  K
H  W  Y  S  L  O  U  I  S  E
B  P  I  N  Q  B  S  N  Y  Q
J  Z  O  R  G  V  F  P  T  V
F  O  L  K  R  D  K  X  H  D
```

Frédéric Chopin was born in the country of _____.

At the age of four, he was taught to play a Bach menuet by his sister, _____ _

Many of Chopin's compositions were based on Polish _____ tunes and songs.

Chopin wrote most of his compositions for solo _____.

Stephen Foster... a composer from the UNITED STATES who lived during the ROMANTIC period of music...

Unit 7

Stephen Foster was born on July 4, 1826 in Pittsburgh, Pennsylvania.

Stephen's father, William, was an important leader in the community. He gave land to help start the community of Lawrenceville in Pennsylvania. For a time, he was a state legislator and a mayor.

His parents provided a happy home life for Stephen, but they lost much of their money when their blank closed in 1832.

Stephen's musical abilities were not particularly encouraged by his parents. They were afraid he could not support himself with a musical career.

Stephen taught himself to play the piano and to read and write music.

In 1850, he married Jane McDowell, a doctor's daughter. They had one daughter, Marion, whom he adored.

He died in New York City at the age of 37.

Stephen, the Gentle Dreamer

"Stevie, please listen! You must learn your spelling words," said Etty, Stephen's older sister.

Trying to help her little brother with his lessons took a lot of patience. Stephen would just smile sweetly and continue to hum the songs that were always in his head.

"All right Etty, I'll try," said Stephen with a sigh.

But thoughts and sounds of the banjos, drums and melodies he heard during the day, kept drowning out the sound of Henrietta's voice as she called out the spelling words.

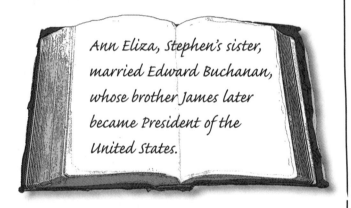

Ann Eliza, Stephen's sister, married Edward Buchanan, whose brother James later became President of the United States.

Stephen's mother was sitting at her desk writing a letter to William, her oldest son. She was telling William about Stephen marching around carrying a drum, wearing a feather in his cap, whistling and singing tunes. Some of the tunes she had never heard before. "There is something totally original about him," she wrote.

Indeed, Stephen was original. He was different from his seven older brothers and sisters. Among his friends, he was respected for standing up for himself and others. He was well behaved and a very intelligent stu-dent. He just didn't like to spend his time studying. He preferred rambling alone through the woods and along the riverbank near his home, his head full of thoughts. The rustling leaves, chirping of the birds and rippling of the water were sounds that soothed his sensitive soul.

His favorite thing to do was to listen to the singing of the hired hands as they worked around his parents' home. He also went to the docks to hear the chanting and singing as the men loaded the riverboats.

He often went to church with their maid, Olivia, who was just a little older than he. His heart was touched as he listened to the beautiful and sometimes sad melodies. He was delighted with the happy and lively rhythm of some of the songs.

One summer, when Stephen was eleven years old, his mother said, "Children, let's get packed. We are going to visit Uncle Struthers!"

The children were all excited. Uncle John Struthers had been a surveyor and hunter in pioneer days. Even though he was an old man now, he loved having the children come for a visit. He told stories of wonderful and exciting adventures. He always let Stephen do just what he wanted.

One day, during their stay at Uncle Struthers, Stephen seemed to be missing. They looked everywhere, and finally found him in a pile of hay in the barn, watching the chickens and other animals and thinking.

Old Uncle Struthers said, "That Stephen is a real original . . . a real original. He will probably be a famous man one day."

Stephen did become famous. He was one of America's most beloved songwriters. His songs are probably better known in the United States and worldwide than any other writer of folk music. He was the first musician to be nominated to the Hall of Fame for Great Americans. He was truly an original.

Stephen Foster composed over 200 songs.

When Stephen died, they found a slip of paper in his pocket that read, "Dear friends and gentle hearts." Maybe this was the title of a song he planned to write, but it describes the character of Stephen himself.

Important Compositions

Stephen's first composition:
Open Thy Lattice, Love

Two state songs:
My Old Kentucky Home
(Kentucky)
Way Down upon the Swannee River (Florida)

Some best loved songs:
Oh! Susanna
Camptown Races
Beautiful Dreamer
Jeanie with the Light Brown Hair

 8

Oh! Susanna

This song was Foster's first great hit and it started his career. *Oh! Susanna* became so popular soon after it was published in 1848, that it became a theme song for the settlers going west to look for gold in California. *Oh! Susanna* was originally written as a song to be sung. On this recording you will hear a transcription for fiddle, banjo and guitar.

Foster Puzzle

Draw a line through the incorrect answer.

Stephen Foster was born in (USA, Canada).

Stephen was taught to play the piano and to write music by (Chopin, himself).

As a boy Stephen liked to (study his lessons, walk in the woods).

Stephen wrote over (20, 200) folk songs.

Stephen Foster was America's first great composer of (folk, rock) songs.

Color the Banjo.

Antonín Dvořák ... a composer from CZECHOSLOVAKIA who lived during the ROMANTIC period of music ...

Antonin Dvořák was born in Czechoslovakia in 1841.

Antonin was the oldest of nine children. Antonin's father, František, was a butcher and innkeeper who played the zither for fun.

The family lived in a small quiet village near Prague. Most of the friendly village people were farmers.

Antonin was taught to play the fiddle by a teacher in the village. When his unusual musical ability was discovered, he went to the Prague conservatory to study organ, piano, viola and violin.

When Dvořák was in America, he visited Spillville, Iowa, where a group of people from Czechoslovakia had settled. It was here that he wrote his famous *Symphony No. 9* ("From the New World").

In his compositions, Dvořák combined native folk music with classical ideas. He became one of Czechoslovakia's most important composers.

Dvořák died in 1904 at the age of 62.

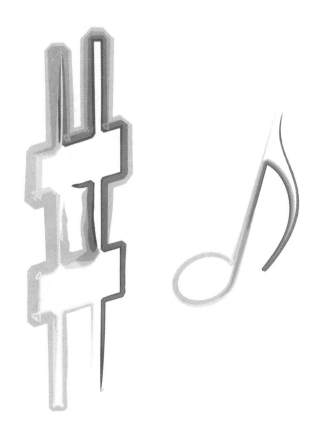

A Simple Czech Musician

Skirts were swirling as the young people danced to the lively music of the town band. The older folks clapped and laughed as the villagers relaxed and had a good time after working in the fields all week.

"Good for you, Antonin," František said to his young son. "You played your fiddle well!"

"Yes," added František's brother Zdenek, "Soon he will be playing his fiddle better than you play the zither!" They all laughed.

"He has such a great talent for music!" All the band members nodded in agreement.

"Well, perhaps we should consider sending him to Prague to study to be a musician," said Zdenek. "What would you think of that, Antonin?"

Before Antonin could answer, his father said, "No, no, no! Antonin will be a butcher like me! He is too young now to leave home anyhow." Fondly, he patted his son on the head.

One day, when Antonin was 13 years old, a letter arrived from Uncle Zdenek. He wrote, "You must let Antonin come to stay with me in Zlonice. Here he can learn the butcher trade and study the German language, which is now spoken in the large cities."

Reluctantly, Antonin's parents sent him to live with his uncle. He did learn the butcher trade, but much to Antonin's delight, he dis-

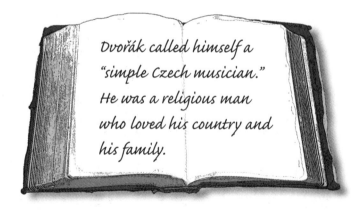

When Antonin was 32 years old, he married Anna Čermáková. They were happily married and had six children.

covered that his German teacher was also the church organist.

Soon Antonin was taking organ lessons along with his other studies. His teacher, Antonin Liehmann, could see right away that Dvořák had an amazing musical talent. Gradually more time was spent on organ, violin, piano, viola and music theory.

Back at home Antonin's parents missed him. One day František hurried into the room where Anna was mending clothes.

"We have a letter from Zdenek," he said.

"How is Antonin?" Anna asked anxiously, as she put away her mending.

"Well it seems that he is doing so well in his musical studies that his teacher is pleading that we send him to study in Prague."

"A musical career?" questioned Anna. "It is so risky, not stable like being a butcher. Where will we get the money?"

Dvořák called himself a "simple Czech musician." He was a religious man who loved his country and his family.

"Zdenek has offered to pay his expenses. I think we must let Antonin follow his heart and study music. After all, if it doesn't work out, he can return home and work with me in the butcher business."

Shortly afterwards, when Antonin was 16, he went to Prague to study. He loved being free to concentrate only on music. As he studied, he was astounded and impressed by the music of the great composers and by the concerts he heard performed by famous musicians.

When he graduated, he received many awards for his own compositions. In them he often used ideas from the popular tunes that he had heard as a boy while playing with the village band.

Many years later,

when Antonin went to America, he was fascinated by the music of the Native American Indian and by the beautiful and haunting melodies of the African-American spirituals. In his famous *Symphony No. 9* ("From the New World"), he used ideas from some of these melodies.

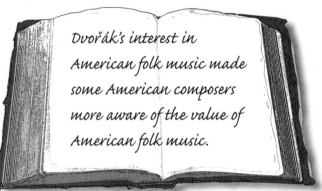

Dvořák's interest in American folk music made some American composers more aware of the value of American folk music.

Important Compositions

Humoresque in G-flat Major, Op. 101, No. 7

Slavonic Dances, Opp. 46 and 72 (Piano Duets)

Symphony No. 9 in E Minor, Op. 95 ("From the New World")

9 ***Symphony No. 9 in E Minor*, Op. 95 ("From the New World"), Second Movement (Largo)**
Dvořák wrote this symphony while he was in America, surely a "new world" to him. His themes were in the style of the American melodies he heard while in America. In 1922, William Fisher wrote words to the Largo movement of this symphony. The verse was entitled "Going Home." It suggests that Dvořák was rather homesick so far away from his homeland.

Dvořák Crossword

Complete the sentences.
Write the answers in the blanks of the puzzle.

1. The first name of both Antonin's wife and mother was _____.

2. Antonin's German teacher also played the _____ in church.

3. Dvořák's famous Symphony No. 9 was called "From the New _____."

4. The first instrument Antonin played

   was the _____.

1. A			

2. | | | |

   N

   T

3. | O | | |

   N

4. | I | | | |

   N

Color this Old World design.

John Philip Sousa ... a composer from the UNITED STATES who lived during the ROMANTIC period of music ...

John Philip Sousa was born in Washington, D.C., in 1854.

His parents came from Portugal to live in America. They provided him with a happy home. His father and older sister taught him to read and write. When he was seven years old, he attended a nearby school.

John Philip also went to music school where he studied violin. When he was 11 years old, he began his own dance band

When he enlisted as an apprentice in the U.S. Marine Band, he studied composition and music theory.

He met his wife Jennie, a singer, while he was on a band tour. John wrote later, "We lived happily ever after."

Sousa's marches made Americans feel very patriotic. His performances inspired many towns to form bands. His distinctly American music was popular throughout the world.

Sousa died in 1932 at the age of 77.

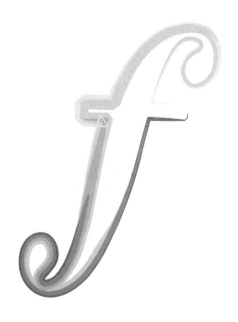

The March King

A large man in a uniform knocked on the door of the Sousa's home in a Washington, D.C. neighborhood. John Philip put down his violin and answered the door.

"Hello! Young man," said the stranger. "I have been listening to your playing for quite a while. You play the violin very well!"

"Thank you, sir," said John Philip. "I play other instruments too."

"Excellent!" said the stranger. "How would you like to play in a circus band?"

"Wow! I would love it!" exclaimed the surprised young boy. "Do you really mean it? A real circus band that travels everywhere?"

"Oh, yes," answered the stranger with a smile. "And we are a very good band too! Why don't you come to the circus grounds tomorrow night? Since we will be leaving town early the next morning, you should bring some clothes in a little suitcase."

"Oh, I know right where that is," said John. "Thank you so much! I'll see you tomorrow night!"

John ran up the stairs and began gathering his clothes together when his mother came into his room.

"And what is all the excitement about, young man? Are you planning to go somewhere?" she asked with a puzzled expression on her face.

"Oh mother, you will never guess! I am going to join the circus and play in the band!"

"Is that so?" asked his mother. "Of course you realize that you will be gone far away from your home and family for many years!"

"Well, I guess so," said John, a little more thoughtful now.

"We'll talk with your father tonight and see what he says," said his mother with a soft smile.

Sousa designed an instrument called the sousaphone (see next page.) It was named for him.

John Philip's father did not smile at all. He was upset to think of this young son leaving to go with the circus.

After talking to John about the hardships of circus life, his father said, "If you would really like to play in a band, I want you to come with me and play in the U.S. Marine Band."

"That is better yet!" said John Philip. "I can play in the band and be at home at the same time!"

The movie Stars and Stripes Forever, made in 1952, was based on John Philip Sousa's life.

John Philip loved playing in the band. He was so good that by the time he was 23, he was named the 14th conductor of the U.S. Marine Band.

The U.S. Marine Band became famous. They played for presidents and kings. John Philip became known as the "March King."

One day, when he was much older, he saw the caravan of a circus traveling to another city. "How glad I am that I joined the marine band with my father, instead of running away with the circus band," he thought. "Had I joined the circus, I never would have become the 'March King'."

Sousa's marches are still played today by many high school, college and concert bands.

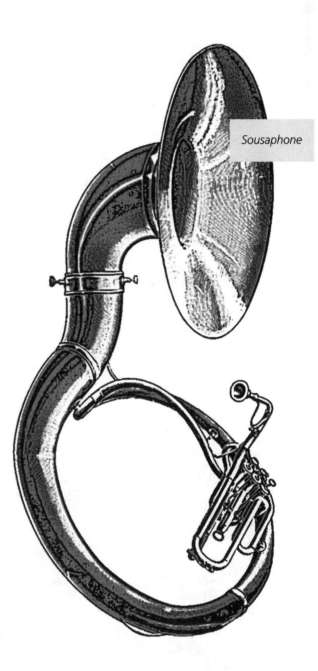

John Philip Sousa composed 136 marches

Sousaphone

Important Compositions

Stars and Stripes Forever

Semper Fidelis

The Washington Post

10 Stars and Stripes Forever

This is one of the most popular marches ever written. In 1897, Sousa was visiting Italy when he got a letter saying a close friend had died. He decided to return home. During the trip home, the melody of this march kept going through his mind. As soon as he got home, he composed the piece.

Sousa Match

Draw a line to connect the circle with the square that matches.

Washington, D.C.

Violin

Sousaphone

the Circus

The first instrument that Sousa learned to play

Sousa's birthplace

Sousa almost joined

Instrument named for Sousa

Military marching band

Edward MacDowell

...a composer from the UNITED STATES who lived during the ROMANTIC period of music...

Edward MacDowell was born in New York City in 1860.

His father was a successful businessman.

Edward's first piano teacher was a friend of the family. He was so impressed by Edward's musical abilities that he introduced him to a well-known concert artist, Teresa Carreño, who taught him—between her concert tours—for a few years.

When he was 15, Edward's mother took him to Paris to study with Antoine François Marmontel who had also taught Claude Debussy. Here he prospered and grew to be an exceptional pianist and an admired composer.

After their marriage in 1884, Edward and Marian Nevins lived in Germany for a few years before retur   heir homeland, the United St

Edward composed many of his works in a cabin that was in the woods just outside of Peterborough, New Hampshire. After MacDowell died in 1908, at the age of 47, he was buried in the woods near the work cabin.

In his memory, Marian made the property into the *MacDowell Colony*. She invited composers, writers and other artists to come to this peaceful place to compose, write or paint.

MacDowell was America's most famous composer of classical music.

The cabin where MacDowell composed

Courtesy of the MacDowell Colony

An Interesting Piano Student

"I am very grateful to you for recommending me as a piano teacher for Miss Nevins," wrote Edward MacDowell to his composition teacher, Joachim Raff. "Although I must admit, I am really not very interested in having female students," he continued. "I find that they are generally not serious about piano, particularly American girls."

He put down his pen and rose to answer the door. At the door was a very beautiful young lady.

> As a boy, Edward liked to draw and read fairy tales. On many of his composition manuscripts, he drew little pictures.

"I am Miss Nevins. Are you the piano teacher, Edward MacDowell?" she asked.

When the stunned Edward nodded, she continued. "Mr. Raff recommended you to be my piano teacher, but I am not so sure about this. You are so young! What are your qualifications?"

"Come in, please," said Edward, when he had finally found his voice. "We will decide what to do. Perhaps we may have a trial period of a few lessons."

That is what was agreed upon, and their lessons began. In fact, their lessons continued for quite some time and they became good friends.

In a letter to Mr. Raff two years later, Edward wrote, "I must admit that I have been pleasantly surprised at the progress of Miss Nevins, whom you recommended to me. She is interested in her studies, and I am pleased to have her as a student."

He continued, "I have finished the composition you assigned me. It is called *Modern Suite No. 1.* I am enclosing the manuscript."

When Mr. Raff looked over the manuscript, he was so excited that he went to see Edward immediately.

"You must take this to Franz Liszt," he said. "I will write a letter to introduce you to this great composer."

Edward traveled to Weimar to visit Liszt, carrying with him the letter from Mr. Raff, the manuscript of the suite and some of his other compositions.

"Young man, this is a very fine suite," said the 75-year-old Franz Liszt. "We must arrange for it to be played in Zurich at a meeting I am attending. I also want you to meet my publisher and see if we can have some of your other compositions published. Play some more for me!"

Edward could not believe his good fortune! "Thank you so much," he said with earnest gratitude to the master composer.

MacDowell's compositions were a great success. In 1884, he proposed marriage to his former piano student, Marian Nevins.

They were a handsome couple. Marian was beautiful, gracious and friendly. Edward had beautiful blue eyes and a handsome, expressive face. He had a good sense of humor, a contagious smile and a lively twinkle in his eye. They were well known and loved in Boston, where he continued performing, teaching and composing. MacDowell became the most important American composer of his time.

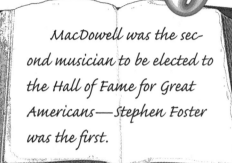

*MacDowell used Native American Indian tunes and rhythms in some of his compositions, such as the **Indian Suite,** Op. 48.*

MacDowell was the second musician to be elected to the Hall of Fame for Great Americans—Stephen Foster was the first.

Important Compositions

To a Wild Rose from *Woodland Sketches,* Op. 51

Indian Suite, Op. 48

Piano Concerto No. 2 in D Minor, Op. 23

11
To a Wild Rose from ***Woodland Sketches, Op. 51***
This suite of 10 musical miniatures may be MacDowell's best known work. *To a Wild Rose,* with its simple melody and fresh harmonies, is probably the most familiar piece from the suite.

MacDowell Word Search

Look down or across to find words that will complete the sentences below. Circle the words.

```
G  O  M  A  R  I  A  N  T  I
J  C  X  E  F  N  A  Z  H  N
H  R  N  K  V  Q  R  G  X  D
R  L  F  B  Q  G  C  I  B  I
L  I  S  Z  T  A  F  P  U  A
P  V  T  E  M  D  L  Y  L  N
D  Y  B  H  L  N  S  G  Q  S
H  U  I  K  J  W  J  A  E  R
V  Z  F  Q  C  D  X  F  W  J
K  M  S  A  M  E  R  I  C  A
```

Edward MacDowell was born in The United States of _____ in 1860.

He had a student, _____ Nevins, whom he later married.

The composer Franz _____ liked MacDowell's compositions and helped to get them published.

MacDowell used tunes and rhythms of Native American _____ in some of his compositions.

Claude Debussy

Unit 11

...a composer from FRANCE who lived during the IMPRESSIONISTIC period of music...

Claude Debussy was born in France in 1862.

As a child, he was rather shy. According to his sister, he would rather watch other children play than join in the fun himself.

At first Claude thought he wanted to be a sailor, because he loved the water so much. However, after having a few piano lessons, he decided that he would much rather be a musician.

When he was eleven years old, he entered the Paris Conservatory. While there, he won many awards for his sight-reading, composition and piano playing abilities.

Claude studied the classical music of the great composers, but he had different ideas in mind for his own compositions. He liked to write pieces that gave an *impression* of the subject he was writing about. He was the first to write these kinds of pieces. He started *impressionistic* music, just as Claude Monet started *impressionistic* art.

Claude Debussy died in 1918 at the age of 55.

A Picnic with Chou-Chou

"Chou-Chou!" called Papa Claude Debussy. "I'm home! Where are you, my little one?"

The six-year-old Claude-Emma, affectionately called "Chou-Chou" (little cabbage) by her father, came into the room and ran to hug him. "Papa, did you remember the picnic?" she asked as she hugged his neck.

"Well of course I did," he said, "just as I promised. Has nurse packed something for us to eat?"

Just then Miss Gibbs, the governess, came in with a basket of chicken, bread, cheese, fruit and cookies.

"Yummy!" said Chou-Chou. "That looks delicious," said Claude.

"Would you like me to go with you, sir?" asked Miss Gibbs.

"If you will, please," said Claude. "I may need some help with Chou-Chou since I promised that we would launch her new toy boat."

Soon they were ready and on their way out the door.

"Oh no! Wait!" cried Chou-Chou. "I forgot Jimbo!"

"I'll find him," said Miss Gibbs. "We must not leave Jimbo behind!"

Debussy loved cats. He had several over the years. He named them all "Line," (pronounced "Lean").

She soon returned with the stuffed toy elephant, which Chou-Chou hugged tightly as they continued on their way.

It was a beautiful, sunny day. They found a grassy spot under a tree by the bank of the river.

They watched the little boat as it floated at the edge of the river and laughed as it turned over time and time again. Chou-Chou and her father took turns seeing who could make the little boat float the farthest without turning over. What a good time they had!

After eating their lunch, it was time to go home.

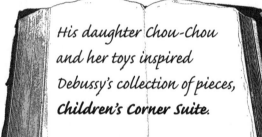

*His daughter Chou-Chou and her toys inspired Debussy's collection of pieces, **Children's Corner Suite**.*

As they walked to the carriage, Claude said, "When we get home, papa wants you to get your bath and put on your pajamas, then I'll have a little surprise for you!"

Chou-Chou was so excited that she wiggled and fidgeted all through the bath. When she got downstairs, her papa lifted her into a comfortable chair and then began to play a piano piece for her.

"This is a piece I wrote for you and Jimbo," he said. "It is called *Jimbo's Lullaby*. It's about you and Jimbo playing. At the end, there is a lullaby for you to rock Jimbo to sleep."

"Jimbo did you hear? Papa has written a piece just for us!" said Chou-Chou with a happy smile.

Her hands moved Jimbo around in a little dance on her lap as she listened to the music.

When the piece was over, Papa Debussy turned around and asked, "Did you like the lullaby for Jimbo, Chou-Chou?"

But there was no answer. Chou-Chou was sound asleep with Jimbo held tightly in her arms. Her papa picked her up gently, carried her upstairs and tucked her lovingly into her bed.

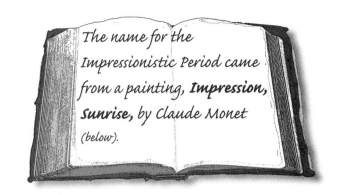
The name for the Impressionistic Period came from a painting, *Impression, Sunrise,* by Claude Monet (below).

CLAUDE MONET

Impression, Sunrise, *the inspiring painting by Claude Monet*

Important Compositions

Children's Corner Suite
(for piano)

Clair de lune
(for piano)

La Mer
(for orchestra)

12
Jimbo's Lullaby from *Children's Corner Suite*

Jimbo, one of Chou-Chou's most-prized possessions, was a little stuffed elephant. In *Jimbo's Lullaby,* Chou-Chou is reading a bedtime story to her favorite toy. As she reads, she gets sleepier and sleepier. She finally falls asleep in the middle of telling the story. At the end of the piece, Debussy wrote the music to be played quieter and slower to give the impression of his little girl sleeping.

Debussy Puzzle

Draw a line through the incorrect answer.

Claude Debussy was born in (Poland, France).

When he was a boy, Claude first thought he would be a (sailor, policeman).

He had a daughter, whom he fondly called (Chou-Chou, Pumpkin).

Debussy liked (dogs, cats).

Debussy's compositions were in a different musical style,
which was called (classical, impressionistic).

Color Debussy.

46

Sergei Rachmaninoff

... a composer from RUSSIA who lived during the ROMANTIC period of music...

Sergei Rachmaninoff was born in 1873 in Russia.

His father was a wealthy retired army officer, and his mother was the daughter of a general.

Sergei had a cousin who was a concert pianist. He suggested that Sergei be sent to Moscow to study piano with Nikolay Zverev. Sergei's parents agreed and sent him to Moscow.

After graduating from the Moscow Conservatory with honors and awards, Rachmaninoff became known as an excellent concert pianist, conductor and composer. It was rare for a musician to be outstanding in all three areas.

In 1902, he married Natalya Satina. They had a daughter, Irina.

He and his family came to The United States. He gave concerts and did some recording for the Victor Talking Machine Company.

Rachmaninoff's final years were spent in California, where he died in 1943 at the age of 69.

Letters from Sergei*

In the fall of 1885, 12-year-old Sergei wrote to his mother:

Dear Mother,

I am happy to be studying music here in Moscow, but my life is very hard! Mr. Zverev, our teacher, makes us get up so early. We begin practice at 6:00 in the morning! Can you believe that?

Maximov and Pressman are living here too. Maxie and I had to pull the covers off of Pressman and pour water on his face to wake him up. He was not too happy with us, but he would have been in real trouble had he been late!

We practice scales and exercises, and then we play duet arrangements of the symphonies. But on Sunday afternoons we have a really good time! Some friends of Mr. Zverev's come here to his home and perform for each other. Last Sunday Mr. Anton Rubinstein came, and next Sunday (the most wonderful news) the great composer and pianist Peter Tchaikovsky himself will be here. My teacher says that I may play for him if I continue to improve and practice faithfully. You can be sure that I am practicing every minute that I can!

I hope that you are well.

Your son,

Sergei

In the fall of 1888, 15-year-old Sergei wrote:

Dear Mother,

I received your letter requesting that I come home after my disagreement with Mr. Zverev. I cannot understand why he was so angry when I asked for a separate room with a piano of my own. I do want to become a concert pianist, but I

also like very much to compose, which Mr. Zverev does not seem to understand. It was simply not possible to concentrate on composing while hearing the other students practice. I just had to leave his home.

I stayed with a friend for a while, but I did not want to impose on him. You will be happy to know that I visited Aunt Varvara Satina, Father's sister, and she warmly welcomed me to live with her and her family.

This is where I am now and I hope to continue composing. Please understand why I cannot come home. I need to stay here to be close to both Rubinstein and Tchaikovsky, whom I admire so much.

Your son,

Sergei

In the fall of 1892, 19-year-old Sergei wrote:

Dear Mother,

I am writing to tell you that I have graduated from the Conservatory. The judges, one of whom was Tchaikovsky, awarded me the Great Gold Medal of the Conservatory. I was very surprised and happy.

You will also be interested to know that Mr. Zverev has come to see me and we

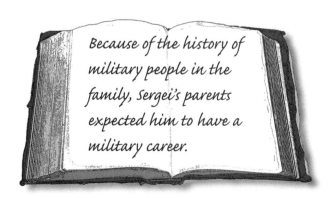

Because of the history of military people in the family, Sergei's parents expected him to have a military career.

*Although Sergei did actually write letters to his mother, these letters are fictional.

have again become good friends. In fact, he introduced me to a publisher who immediately wanted to publish some of my compositions.

I have been giving a number of concerts. The audiences seem to really like a new prelude I have written, which they are calling "The Bells of Moscow." I am also beginning to work on a piano concerto.

Your son,

Sergei

In the spring of 1902, 29-year-old Sergei wrote:

Dear Mother,

There is such good news! My Second Piano Concerto has become a great success. It is praised by almost everyone.

But the best news is that I have become engaged to Mary Natalya Satina. We will be married May 12. We do hope that you can come.

With great joy,
Your son,

Sergei

When the communist government took over, Rachmaninoff left Russia, never to return.

Important Compositions

Prelude in C-sharp Minor,
Op. 3, No. 2

Piano Concerto No. 2 in C Minor,
Op. 18

Rhapsody on a
Theme of Paganini, Op. 43

13
Prelude in C-sharp Minor, Op. 3, No. 2
This is one of Rachmaninoff's most popular pieces. It was called *The Bells of Moscow* by the public, but Rachmaninoff himself denied that it is descriptive in any way.

Rachmaninoff Crossword

Complete the sentences. Write the answers in the blanks of the puzzle.

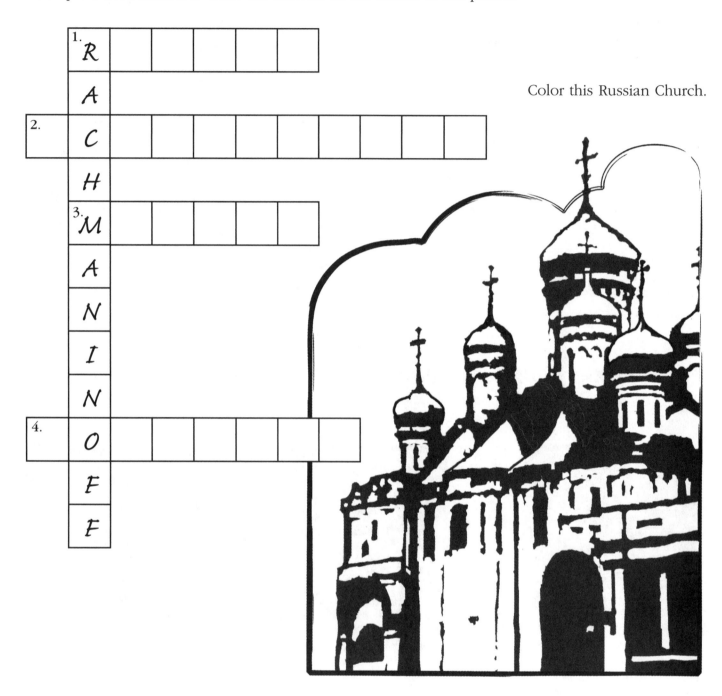

Color this Russian Church.

1. R
A
2. C
H
3. M
A
N
I
N
4. O
F
F

1. Sergei Rachmaninoff was born in _____ in 1873.

2. Sergei admired and respected the great composer Peter _____.

3. Sergei composed a popular prelude called "The Bells of _____."

4. Rachmaninoff was an excellent pianist and conductor as well as a _____.

Composer Game

Rules for Play

On a flat surface, place the composer picture cards face up. The teacher will hold the composer clue cards.

The teacher designates a student to have the first turn, then play continues around the circle.

The teacher reads the first sentence on the clue card and stops. If the student can identify the composer from the first clue, he/she receives the number of points listed on the clue card after that clue. If the student cannot identify the composer, the teacher continues to read clues until the student can identify the composer. If, after all the clues are read, the student still cannot identify the composer, play goes to the next student using the next clue card.

When the student identifies the composer, he/she picks up the composer picture card and keeps it until the end of the game.

Each student keeps a record of the points he/she receives. The student with the most composer cards receives an additional 50 points. The student with the most points wins the game.

Composer Clue Cards (Cut Apart)

Clue 1. This composer was born in Germany in 1685. (20 points)

Clue 2. He came from a family of musicians. (15 points)

Clue 3. He had 20 children. (10 points)

Clue 4. His parents died when he was 10 years old, and he went to live with his brother. (5 points)

(Bach)

Clue 1. These composers were born in Germany in the early 1800's. (20 points)

Clue 2. Both wrote many songs and piano solos called *Song Without Words*. (15 points)

Clue 3. They died the same year. (10 points)

Clue 4. They were very close friends as well as brother and sister. (5 points)

(Mendelssohns)

Clue 1. This composer was born in Austria in 1732. (20 points)

Clue 2. He sang in a boy's choir in Vienna. (15 points)

Clue 3. He had a good sense of humor. (10 points)

Clue 4. He wrote the "Farewell" and "Surprise" Symphonies. (5 points)

(Haydn)

Clue 1. This composer was born in Poland in 1810. (20 points)

Clue 2. He left Poland because of war and could never return. (15 points)

Clue 3. He wrote beautiful pieces for piano including *Military Polonaise*. (10 points)

Clue 4. He carried a jar of Polish soil when he traveled. (5 points)

(Chopin)

NOTE TO TEACHERS: Begin playing the game as soon as two or three composers have been studied. Add others as they are taught.

Clue 1. This composer was born in France in 1862. (20 points)

Clue 2. He was an impressionistic composer. (15 points)

Clue 3. He wrote *Clair de lune* and *Jimbo's Lullaby.* (10 points)

Clue 4. He had a daughter named Chou-Chou. (5 points)

(Debussy)

Clue 1. This composer was born in the United States in 1854. (20 points)

Clue 2. He almost left home to play in a circus band. (15 points)

Clue 3. He played in the U.S. Marine Band and soon became the director. (10 points)

Clue 4. He was known as the "March King." (5 points)

(Sousa)

Clue 1. This composer was born in Russia in 1870. (20 points)

Clue 2. His parents expected him to be a soldier. (15 points)

Clue 3. He admired the great composer, Peter Tchaikovsky. (10 points)

Clue 4. He wrote the very popular *Piano Concerto No. 2 in C Minor.* (5 points)

(Rachmaninoff)

Clue 1. This composer was born in the United States in 1860. (20 points)

Clue 2. He was America's most famous composer of classical music. (15 points)

Clue 3. He became a teacher to a young lady, who later became his wife. (10 points)

Clue 4. He wrote *To a Wild Rose* and *Indian Suite.* (5 points)

(MacDowell)

Clue 1. This composer was born in Germany in 1770. (20 points)

Clue 2. He was a great pianist. (15 points)

Clue 3. He wrote nine very popular symphonies. (10 points)

Clue 4. In his later life he became deaf. (5 points)

(Beethoven)

Clue 1. This composer was born in the United States on July 4, 1826. (20 points)

Clue 2. He had trouble thinking of anything but music. (15 points)

Clue 3. He was America's most famous writer of folk songs. (10 points)

Clue 4. He wrote over 200 songs, including *Oh! Susanna.* (5 points)

(Foster)

Clue 1. This composer was born in Austria in 1797. (20 points)

Clue 2. He was friendly and likeable. His friends called him "Tubby." (15 points)

Clue 3. He wrote over 600 songs. (10 points)

Clue 4. He wrote the *Unfinished Symphony.* (5 points)

(Schubert)

Clue 1. This composer was born in Czechoslovakia in 1841. (20 points)

Clue 2. As a boy, he played the fiddle in the village band. (15 points)

Clue 3. He came to America and was fascinated with the folk music. (10 points)

Clue 4. He wrote the symphony "From the New World." (5 points)

(Dvořák)

Composer Picture Cards (Cut Apart)

Bach

Beethoven

Chopin

Debussy

Dvořák

Foster

Haydn

MacDowell

Mendelssohns

Rachmaninoff

Schubert

Sousa